A Nation of Poets

A Nation of Poets

Writings from the Poetry Workshops
of Nicaragua

Translated with an Introduction
by Kent Johnson

West End Press
1985

Some of the material contained in this book has previously appeared in the following publications: *The Milwaukee Shepherd*, *Arbeiterkampf* (West Germany), *New York Nicaragua Support Bulletin*, *The Minnesota Review*.

ISBN 0-931122-40-6

West End Press, Box 291477, Los Angeles, CA 90029

Table of Contents

Front cover photo: Three women stand before a wall in Tipitapa, near Managua, on which are written the lines of a poem by Leonel Rugama: "The heroes, our heroes, never said they would die for their country; they just died. . . ."

Rear cover photo: Militiaman, near the front. On his hat is written: "I look for Contras."

Photography: Margaret Randall

This book is dedicated to the many Nicaraguan poets who have fallen since the Revolution, defending the sovereignty of their nation; to Oscar Erickson (1903 – 1985) of Fort Bragg, California, lumberjack, union organizer, conservationist, victimized by McCarthyism, tireless worker for peace; and to my son Brooks— when he is old enough, may these simple poems help him understand the common humanity that binds us all.

Poetic Democracy in Nicaragua

Interview: Ernesto Cardenal

2

Poetic Democracy in Nicaragua

In Latin America, Nicaragua has long been known as the "Land of the Poets." Nicaraguans take the title seriously. In the streets of Managua, Granada and Leon, writers are matter-of-factly greeted as "poeta" in the same way that physicians are greeted as "doctor" or priests as "padre."

The country of Ruben Dario (the father of the Modernist Movement of the late 19th and early 20th centuries) has produced such poets as Salomon de la Selva, Jose Coronel Urtecho, Pablo Antonio Cuadra, Carlos Martinez Rivas and Leonel Rugama—writers who, although little known in the U.S., are highly regarded throughout the Spanish-speaking world. To this list we must add the name of Fr. Ernesto Cardenal, Latin America's most famous living poet and Minister of Culture of the Government of Nicaragua.

Following the triumph of the Sandinista Revolution over the Somoza dictatorship in July of 1979, the new Ministry of Culture, under Cardenal's direction, launched an original and ambitious program: to establish "Talleres de Poesia"—Poetry Workshops —across Nicaragua, in poor neighborhoods, factories, agricultural cooperatives, police headquarters and military barracks. The idea had an antecedent. In 1976, at Cardenal's commune in Solentiname on the island of Mancarron in Lake Nicaragua, the Costa Rican poet, Mayra Jimenez, decided to try out a poetry workshop for the inhabitants. The experiment achieved surprising success. Many beautiful poems, since collected and translated into many languages, were written by the campesinos of Solentiname until the commune's destruction by the National Guard in 1977.

The post-insurrection experiment has also surpassed the most optimistic expectations. As many as 70 workshops (the per capita equivalent in the U.S. of about 7,000) have functioned throughout Nicaragua at one time. Hundreds of machinists, peasants, carpenters, street vendors and soldiers, under the direction of a Ministry delegate, have met on a weekly basis to discuss, criticize and write. Regular contests and public readings are held, as well as a weekly national radio show devoted to the workshops, where invited poets read and discuss their writing. Their best work is published every three months in *Poesia Libre*, the national magazine of the Poetry Workshops, as well as in local mimeographed workshop publications and various periodicals and newspapers.

But the U.S.-sponsored aggression has cut deeply into all areas of Nicaraguan life, and poetry is no exception. Since mid-1983, when the "contra" war reached intensified levels, the number of regularly functioning workshops has been reduced to around 30. As Ernesto Cardenal has explained:

> To defend the revolution is to defend poetry as well. . . . Without the Revolution, there would be no possibility of a real grassroots literary movement in this country. And of course, the war has hurt the Workshop program greatly. Many of our best writing instructors have volunteered for the front as have large numbers of the participants. This has brought the number of Workshops down to around half the number we usually had in the three years of relative peace following the triumph. In the past year, a number of the Workshop poets have lost their lives defending the Revolution. . . .
> —*Conversation with the author, December, 1984*

In the late 1950s a circle of poets, led by Cardenal and Urtecho, gave the name "exteriorismo" to the style of poetry they had been writing, deeply influenced, ironically enough, by 20th century U.S. poetry, notably the work of Ezra Pound and the precepts of the Imagist movement. By the late 1960s, "exteriorismo" had become the dominant poetic style in Nicaragua and its leading proponents were directly associated with the rising anti-dictatorial movement. In defining "exteriorismo" Cardenal has said:

> It is poetry made of the images of the exterior world, the world which is seen and palpable, and which is in general the specific world of poetry. Exteriorismo is objective poetry: narrative and anecdotal, made with the elements of real life and with what is concrete, with personal names and precise details,

exact occurences and number, facts and statements. In sum, it is a poetry of the "Impure."
—Introduction, *Poesia Nicaraguense*, Managua, 1975

As the principles of "exteriorismo" are emphasized in the workshops, the vast majority of poems coming from them fall within its stylistic framework. Analogous in significant ways to the "naive" painting movement presently flourishing in Nicaragua, the poetry tends to be anchored in the details of daily life, of unassuming simplicity and directness, and, because it uses the "seen and palpable" world as a central reference, often has an openly political character.

Of course, there is nothing new in Latin America about politically committed literature. From Marti to Neruda there is a long and established tradition. Recently, however, as part of the open and often passionate debate taking place in Nicaragua on the role of culture in the revolution, a number of writers have criticized what they feel is an excessive frequency of political themes in the workshop writing, voicing concern that "social content" may become confused with esthetic value. While such concerns are relevant given the experience of official culture and the fate of artistic freedom in other 20th century revolutions, it seems hardly surprising that at present much of the new poetry is unabashedly political. The interaction of culture and politics is best understood as a natural consequence of the historical situation in Nicaragua: The pains, conflicts and joys of revolution are an inseparable part of Nicaraguan reality, and the poets who choose to deal honestly with these themes are expressing feelings immediate to their own lives and the lives of others.

It is important to point out that Cardenal and leaders of the Sandinista National Liberation Front have explicitly rejected any possibility of "socialist realism" being adopted as official state policy in the arts. The FSLN originated and developed as an independent Marxist organization, breaking with the traditions of Stalinism and seeking to apply an open-ended socialism to Nicaragua's national realities. An important aspect of that political legacy is that artistic freedom is regarded by the Sandinista leadership as a fundamental principle of the revolution. As Daniel Ortega, Nicaragua's President, has put it:

If there is any advice we have [for the artists/artisans], it is that they develop their imaginations, their creative capacities as they themselves see fit. What is needed is to bring up everything that was accumulated and repressed, to develop that without ignoring what there is outside, which will help us develop and move ahead—free of any restrictions whatsoever. To do all this without restrictions, without feeling pressed to give our art a certain tilt in order to stay on good terms with the Revolution. Because we will be on good terms with the Revolution to the extent that we are capable of being ever more creative, of generating new forms, new ideas, of continually exercising our imaginations and breaking with all subservient forms of thinking. Our thinking cannot be shaped by predetermined formulas, it must be completely open. . . .
—From a speech printed in *Hacia una Politica Cultural*, Ministry of Culture, Managua, 1982

The poems in this anthology might be judged by some to be lacking in poetic sophistication. On one level, of course, such criticism would be correct. But polished "form" and "technique" are not prerequisites of artistic merit; and I believe that it is precisely through their lack of literary pretensions and closeness to immediate experience that these poems attain a special freshness and beauty.

Poetry and the arts in Nicaragua are no longer the patrimony of an intellectual elite. Thousands of working class people, many of whom only recently learned to read and write during the Literacy Campaign of 1980, are experiencing newfound joys of poetic and artistic creation. In that process, they are deepening and enriching their enjoyment of life.

This is one more compelling reason why artists and writers in the United States should actively speak out against the senseless war now being waged by the government of our country against the Land of the Poets.

*   *   *

The greater part of these poems were collected in Nicaragua during 1983 while I was working as an Adult Education instructor in basic literacy. With a few exceptions, they are taken from

6

Poesia Libre, the magazine of the Ministry of Culture, and *Antologia de los Talleres de Poesia*, the book-length selection of Workshop poetry published in Managua in 1982.

I am indebted to Father Ernesto Cardenal, Minister of Culture of Nicaragua, and to Julio Valle-Castillo, Director of the Literature Section of the Ministry of Culture and Editor of *Poesia Libre*, for their counsel and encouragement in the undertaking of this project.

I am especially grateful to the Dominican Sisters of Racine, Wisconsin; Sister Barbara Kramer; Pastor Jerome Nilssen; and the Wisconsin Sisters of St. Joan Antida. Their contributions helped make possible a trip to Nicaragua in late 1984, during which the interview with Ernesto Cardenal was conducted.

My thanks to *The Milwaukee Shepherd*, Karen Snider, Ann Kingsbury and Karl Gartung of the Woodland Pattern Book Center, and Professors William Harrold and Jim Hazard of the University of Wisconsin-Milwaukee for their help and encouragement. I am also grateful to Judy Zerger, who expertly typed much of this manuscript, and to my friends Norbert Francis, Ruth Chojnacki, Russell Bartley and Sylvia Yoneda, whose devotion to the cause of non-intervention and social justice in Central America has been a continuous inspiration.

Thanks above all to my wife, Debi Elzinga: Without her countless forms of assistance, this project would not have come to fruition.

—Kent Johnson

Interview: Ernesto Cardenal

I. The Workshops

KJ: The accomplishments of the Ministry of Culture have achieved international recognition. Could you briefly talk about the Ministry, how it was conceived, and some of the tasks it carries out?

Cardenal: In the time of Somoza there was no Ministry of Culture. The revolution created the Ministry when it began to organize the Revolutionary Government in exile. I was asked to become Minister of Culture. We began by establishing Houses of Culture (Casas de Cultura) throughout the country, although a number of them had already been spontaneously set up by the people. Later, the Ministry created regional centers in the main cities. These are the People's Cultural Centers (Centros Populares de Cultura) where amateur artists receive assistance and instruction in music, dance, painting, poetry, ceramics and theater—and where celebrations, exhibits and readings are held. In some ways, these centers function like a town hall in the United States, available to all community or labor organizations who might want to hold an event there.

Great backing has also been given to our traditional crafts and folklore; the new libraries throughout the country and the various cultural publications; the national art schools; the preservation of our cultural heritage; exhibits we bring from other countries as well as the Nicaraguan exhibits we take abroad; the national film institute and its "mobile program," taking movies to the most remote villages in the countryside; and even the promotion of sports and physical education.

KJ: In many countries that are not revolutionary, there are also Ministries of Culture, or at least government institutions that promote culture and the arts. Has the revolution in your country given a new content to the traditional concept of "culture"?

Cardenal: For us, culture and revolution cannot be separated. Everything that belongs to the sphere of culture we con-

8

sider to be within the sphere of the revolution .... and vice-versa. Thus, the term "culture" refers not only to the Fine Arts, but encompasses all those things that define us as Nicaraguans. Of course, our Nicaraguan identity is also, in part, a product of the achievements of other cultures; and it is from this realization that we choose to remain open to the contributions of all world culture, past and present.

Our culture is not elitist, but democratic—a culture by and for the people. But this does not mean that we denigrate the writer, painter or musician who, because of his excellence, necessarily belongs to an elite! Nor does it mean that we believe culture and the arts must be adapted or simplified so that they will be accessible to the masses. What we strive for is a culture of excellence that will be at the same time a culture of the people.

Our vice-president, the novelist Sergio Ramirez, has said that we must "massify" culture. What we really understand by this is the "massification" of excellence.

KJ: It was on the island of Solentiname in Lake Nicaragua a few years prior to the revolution that the famous Poetry Workshops of Nicaragua had their origin. Could you describe how they began and how that experiment became a national program following the overthrow of Somoza?

Cardenal: A poet from Costa Rica, Mayra Jimenez, arrived in Solentiname in 1977. Having had prior experience in Costa Rica and Venezuela with writing programs for children, it occurred to her to try out a Poetry Workshop for the campesinos on the island. She decided to try it with adults, surprised by the fact that despite my having been there some ten years the campesinos had no knowledge at all of my poetry—not to mention modern or classical poetry in general. From the start, they began to write wonderful poems. And hearing of this, a number of important Nicaraguan writers like Jose Coronel Urtecho, Pablo Antonia Cuadra, Fernando Silva, Luis Rocha and others began to visit Solentiname, and were greatly impressed by what they saw and learned from these new poets.

That poetry was published in a book called *Campesino Poetry of Solentiname*, and has been translated and published in many languages.

Upon being named Minister of Culture, it occurred to me to

invite Mayra Jimenez back to Nicaragua to apply on a national scale what she had done at Solentiname. And very soon the workshops began to multiply throughout the country, bringing out many poets who were unknown until then.

KJ: After five years, what is the state of the Workshop program?

Cardenal: There are less now, because many of the instructors and regional organizers have been mobilized in the war. This has hurt the program quite a bit. The war the U.S. government is carrying out against this country affects poetry like everything else . . . most significantly, the aggression has diminished the number of instructors. A number of poets have lost their lives defending this revolution. So I would estimate there are half the number of Workshops we had when the program was at its peak around 1982.

Also, the number of Workshops has fluctuated naturally, as very few are permanent. When the participants have acquired a level of competence and confidence to write on their own without regular instruction and group discussion, then that Workshop is dissolved and a new one is founded in another place. In the army and police force that has happened often— one is dissolved and another is founded in a new barracks or station.

On the average, there have been about seventy Workshops functioning at one time throughout the country. At present, as I told you, there are probably half that number. And the number of people who have participated in the Workshops I calculate to be about 2,000.

KJ: Could you describe the teaching and learning that takes place in a Workshop?

Cardenal: It's not that different from the method used in a poetry workshop on a college campus in the U.S., with variations, of course. Announcements are posted and broadcast, inviting all those interested in poetry—those, that is, who want to write but don't feel they know how, or those who do write and feel they can improve their skills. On the first day, a number of poems are selected by the instructor and read, and the group is then asked if anyone has any poems with them they'd like to read. The poems are analyzed line by line, word by word, and each person gives her or his opinion. In the course of the discussion, the participants begin to discover, among other things, that there are many words or phrases that are unnecessary, simply rhetorical, poorly selected. In this process, revisions are made. As long, that is, as the author accepts the group's suggestions—and it is usually the case that the author changes the text after the group's criticism, although often the author does decline to revise what has been written.

This is a process which can be lengthy, with an hour or more spent on a single poem. With time, many participants begin to present texts that need little or no revision.

In the beginning, the participants are given some general principles. I call these principles "rules," using the term with full knowledge that it might provoke the misunderstanding that we are attempting to impose a certain method and style of writing. I wish to impress upon those holding a casual attitude toward writing that the composition of good poetry is a rigorous exercise and not a pastime . . . that it requires study and the acquisition of technique. In this, I am following Pound's example, who spoke of the "ABC's of Reading."

So these "rules" of mine are directly derived from Pound, but put into terminology that can be understood by the workers and peasants. Because the Poetry Workshops were created for the workers and peasants of our country; they were not created for university students nor for those who, because of their upbringing, are "cultured" in the traditional sense of the word.

What are these rules? In more or less general terms, they call for the preference of the concrete to the abstract; for not binding oneself to imposed patterns or rhymes that can limit poetic expression—in other words, traditional meter; for avoiding unnecessary words; for referring to the things, places and people familiar to the poet by their common names; and for paying attention to one's senses, given that poetry arrives essentially through the ear, the eye, touch, taste and smell.

These guidelines have the intention of helping to overcome some of the difficulties and inhibitions which the beginning writer is naturally confronted with. In no way are they offered with the intention of imposing a single method or style on the participants.

KJ: Aren't these principles of composition also fundamental principles of the literary movement dominant in Nicaragua for the past 30 years—Exteriorism?

Cardenal: Our primary aim in the Workshops is not to build or reinforce any particular "movement." It is to bring the joys of poetry to people who never had the chance to enjoy it before. It just so happens that, having been appointed Minister of Culture and, poetry having become my profession after much study and work, I was in the position to try to share my experience through the Poetry Workshops. If I had been a professor of creative writing at a university in the U.S. or Latin America, I would have taught the techniques and methods that I had acquired through the years. In my position as Minister of Culture, I have done simply that—teach the techniques that I know and believe in to those who have the desire to experience the world of poetry.

KJ: In the past five years there have been numerous and often heated debates among artists in Nicaragua, concerning culture and art in the revolution. One of those debates was focused around the Poetry Workshops. Many writers identified with the revolutionay process have criticized the program, maintaining that the poems coming out of it were too uniform in style, overly didactic and superficial in a political sense. What is your opinion of those criticisms and what was the result of the debate?

Cardenal: Many offered their opinions, and all those who did were poets and writers who support the revolution. They made their criticisms for the most part in the official organ of the Sandinista Front; in Ventana, the literary supplement of Barricada. But there were also criticisms that were not formulated in exactly constructive ways.

Actually, some of them were false accusations. Some said that the poets in the Workshops were forced to write poems with an explicitly political or revolutionary theme, and that is false, because anyone who has made even a cursory reading of the Workshops can see that at least half the poems are about other themes—love, nature, sex, other things.

Another criticism was that the Workshop poetry was too uniform in its style. And it can be said that this criticism, on one level, is quite true. But, as Jose Coronel Urtecho has pointed out, if the poetry of the Workshops is uniform, it is so to the same degree that the type of poetry diametrically opposed to it is uniform: the poetry of hermeticism. In fact, an underlying uniformity is characteristic of all periods and movements in poetry: the Romantics, Greek and Latin poetry, the poetry of the T'ang in China, Japanese poetry, the Beats among other North American movements, the medieval Bards or the Spanish Baroque . . . but in any case, as Coronel summed it up, even if the poems do share a similar style, if it is good poetry, so what?

The Cuban writer Fina Garcia Marruz touches on some of these questions. She finds the phenomenon of "uniformity" perfectly logical. She assumes that the poets will gradually and naturally individualize their styles as time goes on. She also points out something which she considers historically unique: that the working people of Nicaragua have begun to appropriate the heritage of "cultured" poetry to better express their own past and present as a people, when [before] the reverse had always been the case: "cultured" poets had appropriated the people's language and poetry to better express their own individuality. Among many, Lorca is a good example of this . . .

Now, as far as the effect that our polemic produced: It was healthy in that it was an expression of the atmosphere of pluralism and freedom of this revolution. There have been many such public debates and straightforward discussions within the field of culture in the past five years. But at the same time, I think the polemic was also harmful, when those who criticized the Workshops used arguments that were sometimes specious and false.

But perhaps the fundamental reason for that debate was a natural one: There are always different tendencies and movements among artists and these are often at odds with each other. This is so in Nicaragua as it is in every other country in the world. Some poets prefer one type of poetry and others another. Some painters believe in one type of painting and others in another. When you combine these natural differences with a country in the throes of revolution, where art and culture come to the forefront and are in a position to play a significant social role, then naturally you are going to have arguments.

KJ: In many Workshop poems, especially those that deal

with nature, like the poems of the campesinos Jose Domingo Moreno and Juan Bautista Paiz, I've noticed a similarity in tone and effect to classical Chinese poetry. Their poems are quiet and clear with delicate and beautiful juxtapositions of natural scenes. Would you say there are similarities between Exteriorism and classical Chinese poetry in terms of the approach toward the composition of the text?

Cardenal: Many have pointed this out and it is easy to demonstrate—that there are indeed similarities between many of the Workshop poems and Chinese and Japanese poetry. Some of the participants have read the verse of these countries, particularly those who have been involved the longest. But you have mentioned as examples two campesino poets who were only recently taught to write during the Literacy Campaign. I don't think they are familiar with Chinese poetry. I think the similarity you find in their case arises out of a natural affinity toward nature that they have as campesinos.

I edited and in part translated an anthology of Primitivist poetry from around the world. Poetry of the Eskimos, the Pygmies, Nomadic tribes of Africa, large quantities of Native North American poetry, of the Scandinavian Lapps, of the natives of Polynesia and the Amazon. And there are significant similarities between all of them and Chinese and Japanese poetry.

Now, it is also true that contemporary Nicaraguan poetry has been influenced by Chinese poetry. In great part this influence has come to us through North American poetry, which was itself influenced by the Chinese through Amy Lowell and most notably Ezra Pound. Not only in my own works, but that of many others as well. All of this has influenced the Workshops to an extent, but I think that the similarity stems fundamentally from a natural affinity.

II. The Poetic Tradition

KJ: In many nations of Latin America, and especially in Nicaragua, poetry has had a social and political centrality unknown in my country. What historical factors have given so much importance to poetry in Nicaragua?

Cardenal: In Nicaragua almost all literary production has been poetic. This characterizes Nicaragua in relation to other nations of Latin America. It's one of the reasons, I suppose, why we have been termed the "Land of the Poets." Why this is so, I don't know . . . it's a tradition of Nicaragua. When one gets down to it, I think it is difficult to understand why one nation has one tradition and another nation a different one. Why did China have such a great poetic tradition for so many centuries, where nearly everyone wrote verse, from courtesans to emperors to military generals? And why did the Bards proliferate in Ireland during the Middle Ages, and Austria produce so many great composers, and Mexico have such a richness in mural art?

KJ: Perhaps it's easier to understand the preponderance of political themes in Nicaraguan poetry and the significant role poetry played as a spiritual and agitational force in the revolutionary struggle . . .

Cardenal: Here one would have to look at not only one reason, but two or three. One of Nicaragua's specific political characteristics was the existence of a tyranny that most poets had a hard time excluding from their work. But I wouldn't say that was the only reason, since other countries in Latin America have had similar dictatorships, with deep political conflicts, and yet have not produced a significant body of work dealing with political themes.

To this it would be important to add the style of poetry predominant in Nicaragua for most of this century which we have given the name "Exteriorism." Better than "Exteriorism," we would call it "concrete" poetry. A poetry of concrete realities, realist and communicative, lends itself to transmit a political or social theme much more naturally than a poetry which is abstract, introspective and instead of communicative, hermetic. How could a poetry of this type be social and political? I think it's almost impossible.

And still another factor is tradition. This tradition has its beginnings in Ruben Dario, who was far from the apolitical aesthete he is often made out to be, engaging contemporary political themes in his verse as in his prose. Following Ruben during the first decades of the century was Salomon de la Selva, one of our great poets, who dealt very much with political themes. Later, in the '20s, come the poets of the Vanguardia Movement, who were very concerned with Nicaragua's national identity, particularly the occupation of our country by U.S. Marines and Sandino's resistance against them. When Leonel Rugama appeared during the '60s, there was already a long and deep tradition of political poetry and the style we call Exteriorismo—that's to say, concrete and realist poetry. Rugama, while continuing in this vein, also broke new ground.

So you see, these new poets in the workshops already have a strong tradition behind them. It is easy and natural for them to write this kind of poetry, while for others, in different countries, it is not.

KJ: You were saying that you felt it was nearly impossible that "abstract" or "hermetic" poetry could carry a social or political content. Nevertheless, there have been poets who have employed non-"realist" styles to communicate, often effectively, a political message. Some of the French Surrealists, for example, during the Nazi occupation, or Vallejo in some of the poems of *Spain, Take this Chalice from Me*. In the United States, during the Vietnam War, many poets, notably Robert Bly, moved thousands of people writing and reading a poetry that expressed the psychic nightmare of that war with surrealist techniques. Don't you think that poetry, as well as the other arts, can educate and inspire in a political sense without being "realist" in style?

Cardenal: Well, I stated I felt it was *almost* impossible that hermetic poetry—which actually by its own definition does not communicate a clear message—could communicate social or political concerns. But I didn't want to be dogmatic. And as in most things of this world, there are exceptions . . . as you mentioned, some of Bly's anti-war poetry, which actually, one might say, revealed the very *real* surrealist terror of that war . . . But I don't agree with you on *Spain, Take this Chalice from Me*, which I regard as a highly sophisticated, realist, concretist poetry, full of the people's spirit, and loaded with political message and even slogans!

I want to make it clear that when I speak of "realism," I am not advocating a type of "socialist realism." In this regard, I am in full agreement with Che Guevara, who said that so-called "socialist realism" was nothing more than a warmed-over version of 19th-century bourgeois "realism." And when I speak of "abstract" or "hermetic" poetry, it's not that I'm in absolute opposition to it. What I understand and mean by "abstract" poetry is that which purposely dissociates itself from the objective world, and in so doing, distances itself from political and social reality. Although, of course, the writer has every right to compose such verse, he shouldn't be under the illusion that he's usually going to inspire a lot of people to action—as some of Latin America's best political poetry has done—or that he's normally going to be persecuted by the policemen of a military dictatorship for writing hermetic verse. I say "normally" because, here too, one can envision exceptions. Especially with those kinds of policemen . . .

KJ: The poetry of the United States has deeply influenced modern Nicaraguan verse. Could you talk a bit about the origins of this influence? The relationship seems a bit ironic given the actual situation! I am thinking also of other revolutions which have deemed it necessary that cultural influences from the "First World" be restricted. This does not seem to be the case in Nicaragua.

Cardenal: Modern North American poetry was introduced here by Jose Coronel Urtecho after returning from the U.S. in 1925. Upon returning he founded the Vanguardia Movement, which from its inception was deeply influenced by the finest poetry being written at that time in the U.S.—by poets like Eliot, Pound, Sandburg, Frost, H.D., Stevens and so on.

Previous to this, Ruben Dario had been aware of the work of Whitman and had even dedicated poems to him. And after that, Salomon de la Selva was influenced so much by English and U.S. poetry that he even began to write in English. His first book was in English, and his work was included in a post-war anthology introducing the most promising young poets of the U.S. He was friends with many poets of the time, including Edna St. Vincent Millay, with whom he apparently had an affair. Soon afterwards he stopped writing in English in protest of Roosevelt's policies toward Latin America. But even thereafter, his verse retains its North American flavor.

Coronel introduced a whole generation to U.S. poetry. And

the following generation was influenced in the same way through a large U.S. anthology that Coronel was putting together and sharing in the process. I was so taken with those poems that I left for the U.S. in 1947 to learn English and study North American literature.

KJ: To Columbia University . . . Did you meet other poets there?

Cardenal: No—Ginsberg was there at the same time I was. We found this out when we first met. We were actually in the same class, but we didn't know each other. Columbia had a student body of 40,000!

Anyway, after I had learned English, Coronel proposed that we put together another anthology which would be even larger and more comprehensive than the one he had previously done. We made a book that was over 400 pages long and begins with the North American Indians and concludes with the Beat poets. We labored some 20 years on the project.

These translations had a deep impact among Nicaraguan poets. And this poetry was also influential in Cuba. Actually, Nicaraguan poetry in general had a big impact in Cuba during the '50s and '60s and through it, directly and indirectly, North American poetry did as well. It can be said that to a significant extent, the work of the most important poets of the Cuban Revolution has evolved under the influence of the best modern U.S. poetry.

Now, as far as your reference to cultural influences from the "First World" . . . our opinion is that North American poetry has nothing to do with imperialism. As revolutionaries, what we understand by "imperialism" are the big multi-national enterprises and the world-wide structure of exploitation they generate. And although in a broad historical sense one should never completely divorce a nation's culture from the economic and social network out of which it has arisen, at the same time we aren't going to draw an equals sign between the poets, dancers, musicians and painters of the U.S. and the multi-national monopolies!

One of your country's great writers, Guy Davenport, has said that since Whitman, the U.S. government has been mistrustful of its poets. And in fact, a large part of great North American verse has been in opposition to the U.S. government and its policies. The only one who in a certain sense was pro-empire was Whitman. But the vision he had of the U.S. was very different from what your country turned out to be later on! He imagined a world-wide republic founded on love and a universal sister- and brotherhood. And I would say almost all the important poets after him have been critical in one way or another of the policies of the U.S. government.

KJ: But that opposition has not been expressed in an obvious way. There is no tradition of committed poetry in my country as there is in Latin America, where social conflicts are apparent and immediate. In fact, I would say that a significant number of U.S. poets consider "political poetry" to be an inferior genre of literature and unworthy of their craft.

Cardenal: But there is a great tradition of progressive poetry in the U.S., from Whitman to Ginsberg! And there have also been very important poets whose work has been quite political, though their politics have been far from laudable: Eliot for example, with his particular brand of ideology . . . Robinson Jeffers, who was actually pro-Nazi, preferring barbarism to civilization, and the animal kingdom to humankind; a declared enemy of Western civilization. That's why he praised the Nazis, because they were barbarians and were going to destroy the civilization he hated . . . a very special case!

The most political of them all, of course, was Ezra Pound. Setting aside his misguided involvement with Fascism and his anti-Semitism, if we take an objective look at his poetry, particularly the Cantos, we find that Pound's verse is deeply anti-capitalist. One of his central themes is the protest against the fetishization of capital—against capital finance and the human suffering it generated. His work is not only social and political in theme, but structured on an economic analysis. In this sense, as paradoxical as it might seem, I think Pound's Cantos come closer to what might be considered a Marxist poetic than any other poetry written in English up until that time.

It's interesting to think what Pound might have been like under different circumstances. Of course, he was such a great and unpredictable genius that it's very difficult to say. But despite the fact that he aligned himself with Mussolini, he also attempted to convince Stalin, through a letter, of his theory of

Social Credit. In fact he went to the length of learning Georgian so that he could compose the letter in Stalin's native tongue! And he attempted to convince Roosevelt, as well as the Spanish Republic through Salvador de Maradiaga. But it happened that Mussolini was the one who most accepted his economic theories. At least that's what Pound believed. Whether or not that was truly the case, I'm not so sure. I doubt it. I find Pound's economic doctrine very complicated but extremely interesting. And although he has not usually been taken very seriously in the past, I've noticed lately that there are some people who are beginning to.

One thing I am sure of, is that if Pound's life had coincided with the Nicaraguan Revolution, he would have tried to convince us of his economic theories in the same way he tried to convince other governments. And I would have asked the companeros of the Ministry of Finance to at least give him a fair hearing. Really, much of what he proposed was diametrically opposed to the policies of the International Monetary Fund, which as you know have contributed to the underdevelopment of Nicaragua and so many other countries of the Third World.

KJ: I wonder if a correlation between a Marxist aesthetic and Pound's poetry might exist at an even more fundamental level. I'm referring to what is implicit in the poetic of "Imagism" and what Pound explicitly formulated in his essay on Gautier Brzeska: that the exterior, material world exists independently of human consciousness, and that the artist is capable of reflecting in an approximate way the real and changing relations of that world. In fact, Pound directly counterposes the poetic of "Imagism" to the obscurities of "Symbolism."

Now you have stated that realist and concretist poetry "has constituted the great poetry of all the ages," and at the same time, that "realist" poetry is the most adequate vehicle to communicate a social message . . . is the option that you and so many Nicaraguan poets have taken for a "realist" poetry based mainly on literary preferences, or on a conscious desire to give poetry a social and political role?

Cardenal: As I have said, I don't exactly like the term "realism" as a description of our poetry, which we called "Exteriorist" and which we really should have called "Concretist." This poetry can be realist or non-realist, or incorporate the various shades and forms of realism.

As far as the attraction of many of us for the "concrete" goes, this stems wholly from our literary preferences and not from a conscious desire to play a social or political role with our verse. Proof of this is that much of this type of poetry in Nicaragua is completely divorced from social or political themes, and deals instead with the individual's most private realm, such as love or eroticism—in my case, sometimes, with what some have called an erotic mysticism. Naturally, most of us in Nicaragua also write social and political poetry. But in a sense this is also due to literary preference: Given that our lives are highly motivated by social and political ideals and finding ourselves as actors in great political struggles, we feel these themes deeply and sincerely, so that the aesthetic and political join quite naturally in our hearts.

But I would also say that the aesthetic results of one who wrote political poetry without sincerity would be as disastrous as one who tried to write a love poem without being in love!

KJ: Could you tell me if the publication and study of U.S. poetry has continued since the revolution?

Cardenal: Although we are limited by the scarcity of paper, printing facilities and translators, North American poets frequently appear in the literary supplements of the daily papers. *Poesia Libre*, our quarterly journal, has also published a North American poet in practically every issue: Whitman, William Carlos Williams, Marianne Moore, Muriel Rukeyser, Ginsberg, Pound, Jeffers, Paul Blackburn, John Ashbery and many others.

KJ: You mentioned Ginsberg. Has his work influenced your writing in any way?

Cardenal: Yes, I have learned a number of things from him. What he's taught me is, in fact, in line with Pound's teaching, from whom he has learned, as have perhaps all contemporary North American poets, consciously or not.

Of course, different poets may assimilate and refine a certain aspect of a master's teaching over other aspects. And in general, the link with a common heritage is developed through a sharing and assimilation of these different refinements. What I have assimilated from Ginsberg is his freedom of expression;

in particular his attention to the details of the everyday world. The mundane, "un-poetic" facts of the modern world which he, more than anyone, had the vision to regard as within the realm of poetry.

There is a poem of his, for example, where with the finest detail he describes flying in an airplane from New York to San Francisco. As he describes what he is seeing from the window, he brings in the music from his earphones, images on the movie screen, things the other passengers are doing around him, as well as the intimate thoughts in his own mind—all of it intermeshed in the most beautiful way, until the poem ends with his friend embracing him at the airport. For those who want to write about the real and actual things of this world, his poems are excellent teachings!

III. Poetry in the Revolution

KJ: I'd like to ask you a question now which I think is important to many artists in other countries. As you know, other revolutions have imposed political and aesthetic norms on artists that have resulted in severely limiting creative freedom. Have the leaders of the Nicaraguan revolution, and the artists aligned with it, studied these other experiences in a critical way?

Cardenal: Yes, and we have seen that it is negative to attempt to limit artistic creativity. More to the point, we have seen that it kills art and stunts the human spirit. This is something that has been made very clear by the leaders of the revolution. Artistic freedom is a fundamental principle of the Nicaraguan revolution. In fact, we could almost say it is a dogma . . . although the term "dogma" might not be such an appealing one! But we could say that freedom of creativity in the arts is a "dogma" of this revolution.

KJ: You say the "comandantes" have this opinion also?

Cardenal: Especially them. Daniel Ortega and Tomas Borge are the ones who have dealt most with the subject of culture among the "comandantes." But as I said, freedom in the arts is a profound principle for us and is shared by all the central leaders of the Nicaraguan government.

KJ: There's a pretty big contradiction between what you have just stated and the accusations of "totalitarianism" directed against Nicaragua by the Reagan Administration . . .

Cardenal: Yes, naturally . . . they have a bizarre conception about this revolution. But we aren't only talking about our declarations. One only has to look at the type of art that is exhibited here, or which the government buys to adorn state buildings, or gives to visiting officials from other countries. There is a multitude of different kinds of art, from realist to the most avant-garde experimental styles. And the same is true in literature, as one can readily verify by looking at the literary magazines or the diverse material put out by the state publishing houses, like Editorial Nueva Nicaragua. In music last year we had a huge festival—political music from all over Latin America—and a few months later put on an international festival of romantic music. Here in Nicaragua there are no borders as far as art is concerned. There are absolutely no restrictions on what comes in or goes out.

KJ: I don't know very much about Nicaraguan painting, but I understand that the most famous artists are abstract painters.

Cardenal: That's correct. The most important one is Armando Morales, who has an international reputation and presently serves as our Ambassador to UNESCO. After him comes Alejandro Arostegui; both are abstract artists. And this is generally true of most of our contemporary professional painters. There are some academic and realist artists who have achieved a fair level of success, but the dominant trend here in the plastic arts is one of avant-garde experimentation. Again—the only official line here as far as the arts are concerned is that there is no official line.

KJ: I'd like to ask you about modern Latin American poetry. In an interview a number of years ago, the late Salvadoran poet Roque Dalton tells the Uruguayan writer Mario Benedetti that he belongs to the "Vallejo Family" of poetry and not to the "Neruda Family." He places himself alongside Juan Gelman, Nicanor Parra, Roberto Fernandez Retamar and Ernesto Cardenal. I'm curious about this, as in the U.S. we tend to place Vallejo and Neruda together as the two giants of socially committed poetry in this century. What is that difference Dalton is referring to?

Cardenal: Well, for us Vallejo and Neruda are very different. Some prefer one and others the other one. In general, the new poets prefer Vallejo over Neruda. Neruda fell too often into highblown rhetoric . . . he wrote too much perhaps. His political concerns often caused him to become too wordy, too agitational in a sometimes ineffective way. Politics figures little in Vallejo's verse, excepting his later poetry of the Spanish Civil War. In general, his poetry was not political in a direct way. Indirectly it was, because he dealt very much with the subject of poverty, the difficulties of life and so on. But he was more a poet of the "inner world" and Neruda more a poet of the "masses," a popular poet.

I was influenced by them both and admired them greatly, until I left them behind to find a different kind of poetry.

KJ: But if Neruda was a "poet of the masses" and Vallejo more concerned with the "inner world," it seems very contradictory that such a socially committed poet as Dalton would declare himself in the tradition of Vallejo as opposed to Neruda!

Cardenal: Things must be placed within their proper chronology. Roque said this many years ago, when he was not yet writing the great poetry he wrote in the few years before his death—which is not in the vein of Neruda or Vallejo, but rather is an exteriorist poetry, directly influenced by Nicaraguan and modern U.S. verse. Roque evolved in his poetry and even has a poem, from his clandestine period, where he pokes fun at his old work . . . he is making fun of a very bourgeois poet and quotes a few hermetic lines to help make his point. In reality, the lines are taken directly from an old poem by Roque himself!

KJ: And what was that "different kind of poetry" you sought, and what experiences led you to search for a different style?

Cardenal: North American poetry. Simply because I saw in it the possibilities of expressing what I wanted to express; with an endless source of themes, taken from real life and with common, everyday speech . . . without having to resort to an outpouring of metaphors like Neruda, whose verse to me was old-fashioned (although in my youth I was an imitator of him), and without having to imitate Vallejo, because Vallejo is such a deeply personal, original poet, that almost no one can be really influenced by him without becoming his imitator.

KJ: Pablo Antonio Cuadra is a Nicaraguan poet who is internationally famous. You were close friends at one time. In fact, Cuadra played an important role in your own promotion as a poet. Now Cuadra, one of the directors of La Prensa, has adopted an anti-revolutionary position. Many people would like to know what your present relationship is. Is there dialogue with those writers who have taken positions contrary to the revolution?

Cardenal: Among major Nicaraguan poets, Pablo Antonio Cuadra's case is a singular one. We weren't only friends, but were like brothers. In fact, we are first cousins, but our love for one another was like brother to brother. And Coronel Urtecho's relationship with him was the same, perhaps even more intimate. As father to son perhaps, because Pablo Antonio was really formed as a writer by Coronel. But when Pablo Antonio turned so drastically against the revolution, our relationship with him came to an end. We have committed ourselves to the revolution with all our hearts and his position has caused a deep separation between us. It has been a number of years now since we have spoken.

KJ: I know this last question is conditioned by what may happen in the coming months and years . . . but given a climate of peace, what is your vision of the future of culture in Nicaragua?

Cardenal: With what the revolution has produced in such little time and under such great difficulties—especially the external aggression and the related economic troubles—with the great successes we have witnessed in such little time, I think we can't even calculate what we could achieve if our country were granted normalcy and peace. And to be honest with you, what we have witnessed already I never imagined possible so quickly. This revolution has been more than I ever dreamed.

And we ask the poets, the artists of other nations, to defend Nicaragua in these difficult times. To defend the right of Nicaragua to live in peace. To do so is to defend culture and poetry as well.

Poems from Solentiname:
1976 – 1977

TO MY FATHER

Whenever I come to visit, sadness overcomes me.
I miss your guidance, the stories
you would tell me about your friends or yourself.
I no longer hear your joyous laughter.
I only know your happiness by your gestures;
you struggle to let me know with the one arm you can still move.
And when I can't understand, you grow solemn,
lower your gaze,
and your eyes are haloed with tears.

Felipe Pena
Solentiname
Killed in the struggle against Somoza

THE SON

I want a son, and to feel the joy
of being a mother.
To wash him every day, dress him,
powder him, give him to drink
and his food at the right hour.
Gaze at him and distinguish who he looks like most—
me or my lover?
Dream that when he has grown
he shall struggle for the freedom of my people.

Gloria Guevara
Solentiname

A MI PADRE

Cada vez que te vengo a ver me entristezco.
Me hacen falta tus consejos, las anécdotas
que me platicabas de tus amigos o tuyas.
Ya no te escucho reír alegre.
Sé que estás contento por el gesto que hacés;
te afanás haciendo señas con la mano que te ha quedado buena.
Y cuando no te entiendo, te ponés serio,
mirás para abajo,
y se te rodean los ojos de lágrimas.

EL HIJO

Deseo un hijo, y el sentirme ser madre.
Bañarlo todos los días, vestirlo,
perfumarlo, darle su refresco,
y su comida a sus horas.
Contemplarlo, y distinguir a quién se parece
¿a mí o a mi amado?
Soñar que cuando esté grande
sea un combatiente por la liberación del pueblo.

ALCOHOLISM

I'm amid stones and the rotting
refuse of my country.
My clothes are filthy and torn,
my shoes have practically vanished.
I'm pale and smelly,
everyone looks at me with scorn.
When I'm really drunk
I sing and yell.
My brother flies keep me company by day
and the mosquitoes suck my blood at night.

Gloria Guevara
Solentiname

U.S. LOGGING COMPANY

They've cut down our oaks, guanacastes,
cedars and laurels.
In the distance
near the source of a stream
a leafy tree still stands
and in its shade, a pale deer.

Ivan Guevara
Solentiname

EL ALCOHOLISMO

Estoy entre piedras y basuras
hediondas de mi pueblo.
Mi ropa está sucia y rota,
mis zapatos ya se terminaron.
Estoy de mal color y maloliente,
toda la gente me mira con desprecio.
Cuando estoy bien embriagado
canto y grito.
Mis hermanas moscas son mi compañía por el día
y los zancudos me chupan la sangre por la noche.

COMPANIA DEL TRANSITO

Cortan robles guanacastes
cedros y laureles.
A lo lejos
al fondo de una quebrada
ha quedado un árbol frondoso
y a su sombra, un venado pálido.

I REMEMBER THAT DAWN

I remember that October dawn
running from the National Guard
after the assault on the San Carlos Garrison
when I began to drown as we crossed the Frio River
and I yelled: Ivan I'm drowning!

Yet the first to reach me was not Ivan
but rather you Alejandro.

Nubia Arcia
Solentiname

THE EGRETS

The large egrets
elegant and white
fish all day long.
They complain and even fight when another
fishes in one's favorite cove.
Each sardine means a flight to the nest
because in its narrow stomach
there is room for only two:
one for its own sustenance and another for its child.

Seen from a distance, an egret
can be mistaken for a Virgin.*

Alejandro Guevara
Solentiname
*una virgen = image of The Virgin.

RECUERDO AQUELLA MADRUGADA

Recuerdo aquella madrugada de octubre
cuando huíamos de la Guardia Nacional
después del asalto al cuartel de San Carlos
cuando me ahogaba al cruzar el río Frío
y grité: —Me ahogo Iván.

Pero no fue Iván el primero en llegar
sino que fuiste vos Alejandro.

LAS GARZAS

Las garzas grandes
blancas y elegantes
pescando todo el día.
Protestan y hasta pelean cuando otra
pesca en su costa favorita.
Cada sardina es un viaje al nido
porque en su estrecho estómago
caben dos
una de su alimento y otra para
un pichón.

Una garza de largo
se puede confundir con una virgen.

Poems from
The *Talleres* in the Revolution:
1979 –

34

TO THE U.S.A.

I visited the tomb of Carlos Fonseca*
and saw the burning torch,
and the flame that rose from that torch
shall never be extinguished by Northern winds.

It shall never be extinguished.

Justo Fernando Vallejos
Literacy teacher
Member of the 19th of July Sandinista Youth Organization
Poetry Workshop of Dario City
*Founder of the Sandinista National Liberation Front

ORLANDO

I remember you son,
brave, reckless,
hoarse from yelling in the marches
with your striped, coffee-colored shirt
the one we keep in our dresser's
second drawer.

Maria Pineda
Factory worker
Poetry Workshop of Condega

A EE. UU.

Yo visité la tumba de Carlos Fonseca
y vi la antorcha encendida,
y la llama que salía de esa antorcha
nunca podrán apagarla los vientos del Norte

nunca podrán apagarla.

ORLANDO

Te recuerdo, hijo,
valiente, atrevido
afónico de tanto gritar en las manifestaciones
con tu camiseta café rayada
la que guardamos en la segunda gaveta.

TO MY MOM

When in April the war caught up with me in Esteli
you would sit in a corner and cry.
You like so many women:
washing, ironing
                    and always pregnant.
That's how you were: pregnant and weeping for me
in a corner.
And when I left shortly after you gave birth
they tell me that you fainted.
Fear of the National Guard made you flee to Honduras.
Later you returned
and were overjoyed to see me.
Now, in this free land, I wanted to tell you mom,
that when I left I did it for you
for all the people
because I love you deeply

Pedro Pablo Benavides
Occupation unavailable
Poetry Workshop of Esteli

THE LAST DAY OF SOMOZA'S LIBERAL PARTY

Pancha had diarrhea,
the baby had an intestinal infection
and Polo had dysentery.
And Pancha swept the floor
and Polo milked the cow
and the baby pulled at his mother's breast.
The whole shack smelled like shit.

Juan Antonio Lira
Regional Delegate of the FSLN
Poetry Workshop of Condega

A MI MAMA

Cuando en Estelí me agarró la guerra de abril
ovs te ibas a un rincón de la casa a llorar.
Vos como tantas mujeres:
lavando, planchando
                    y panzonas siempre.
Así estabas vos: panzona y llorando en un rincón
pensando en mí.
Y cuando me fui
vos recién parida dicen que te desmayaste.
El miedo a la guardia te hizo huir a Honduras,
después volviste
y te alegraste conmigo.
Y ahora en la tierra libre quería decirte, mamá,
que cuando me fuir lo hice por vos
por toda la gente
porque de veras te quiero.

EL ULTIMO DIA DEL PARTIDO LIBERAL NACIONALISTA

La Pancha estaba con diarrea,
el chigüín con la gastroenteritis
y Polo con disentería.
Y la Pancha así barría la casa
Polo así ordeñaba la vaca,
y el chigüín así jalaba el pezón de la mama.
Toda la casa olía a mierda.

38

IN MASAYA

We met in sight
of the Guardia Command post.
Your tennis shoes were covered with mud.
There was a small stain of blood
on my white T-shirt.
You asked me if I was "going to get a haircut."
I answered: "There's chewing gum
                at my aunt's house."
There were Guards all around us.
You embraced me
and self-consciously I walked away.
We were mistaken for lovers.
No one realized our meeting
was a Sandinista contact.

Marvin Rios
Literacy teacher
Member of the 19th of July Sandinista Youth Association
Ernesto Castillo Poetry Workshop

EN MASAYA

Frente al comando de los guardias
nos encontramos.
Vos traías los zapatos tenis lodosos.
Yo en la camiseta blanca
una manchita de sangre.
Me dijiste que si me iba a "cortar el pelo."
Yo respondí la clave: —"donde mi tía
                                hay chicles.́"
Cerca de nosotros sólo guardias.
Vos me abrazaste
y yo nervioso caminé.
Nos confundimos como novios.
Y nadie se dio cuenta
que estábamos en un contacto sandinista.

THE MANAGUA CIRCUS

I remember, Bombon,
in May of 1978, when you fell from the tightrope,
maybe because you were thinking of your ten-year-old sister,
the trapeze artist, who was very ill.
Pale, you held back your tears
and the spectators made fun of you
and laughed and laughed.
That afternoon, after the rainstorm,
was her burial
(only the circus troupe was there).
On her grave, a cross made of tied sticks
and a pale wreath of narcissus.
Two days later, in your clown suit,
you tried a new trick that didn't work.
They booed and threw things at you,
but you calmed them down and made them laugh again.
No one understood you.
That was how it was before the Revolution.

Sergio Vizcaya
Literacy teacher
Militia volunteer
Poetry Workshop of Condega

EL CIRCO ORIENTAL

En mayo de 1978
recuerdo Bombón, cuando caíste de la cuerda floja,
tal vez porque pensabas en tu hermana de diez años
que era trapecista y estaba enferma.
Pálido, no lloraste
y el público reía
se burlaba y reía.
Aquella tarde después de la lluvia
fue el entierro de ella
(sólo los del circo fueron).
En la sepultura una cruz de tigüilote
y una corona de flores pálidas de narciso.
A los dos días, vos vestido de payaso
te presentaste con un truco que no dio resultado
te tiraron muchos objetos
pero los calmaste y los hiciste reír.
Nadie te comprendía,
la Revolución todavía no había llegado.

42

IN SIUNA

A Douglas C-47
lifted off from the field.
I was on my way to the Atlantic Coast mines.
They gave me a copper badge,
a helmet of compressed cardboard,
a twelve-volt lamp.
I was number 259 in the long line
(there were Sumos, Miskitos and Blacks).
In the distance, at the tunnel's mouth,
they were greasing a wagon.
A Yankee asked us our names.
With the others I left my thumbprint.
I spent 7 years melting gold
in the foundry furnace,
inhaling the dust thrown up by the drills
in the tunnels,
seeing the others, like myself,
being consumed by tuberculosis.
They amputated Pantaleon Hernandez's
right leg
and he passes his days sitting in the hallway
                              where I taught him to read.

Carlos Pineda
Former mineworker – presently medical student
Poetry Workshop of Condega

EN SIUNA

Un Douglas C-47
despegó de la pista,
viajaba en avión a las minas de la Costa Atlántica.
Me dieron una placa de cobre,
un casco de cartón comprimido,
una lámpara de 12 voltios,
era el número 259 de la fila de obreros
(habían sumos, miskitos y negros).
Al fondo antes de entrar al túnel
engrasaban un vagón.
Un yankee pedía los nombres.
Con otros dejé la huella digital.
Estuve 7 años derritiendo el oro
en la caldera de fundición,
oliendo el polvo que levantaban los taladros
en los paderones,
viendo a otros que como yo
se consumían por la tuberculosis.
Le amputaron la pierna derecha
a Pantaleón Hernández
y vive sentado en el corredor donde lo alfabeticé.

DURING SOMOCISMO

Empty and rusting cans
of Victoria or Light beer
mixed in with loose pages of Corin Tellado
photonovellas
and pages of *Time* and *Vanidades*
seemed to be sleeping in those mounds of refuse.
And each day loose pages or whole magazines
arrived at the city dump,
joining the empty, rusting cans
of Victoria, Light or Kerns
and empty boxes of Corn Flakes
and in the public toilets there were loose pages
of *Time* to wipe yourself with, along with portraits of Somoza,
which the poor pasted on the folding screens of their homes.

Juan Ramon Falcon
Campesino
Presently studying civil engineering
Ernesto Castillo Poetry Workshop

CUANDO EL SOMOCISMO

Las latas de cerveza Victoria o Light
                    vacías y oxidadas
revueltas con páginas sueltas de fotonovelas
Corín Tellado
y de revistas *Time* o *Vanidades*
parecía que dormían en tanta basura.
Y a diario llegaban al basurero
páginas sueltas o fotonovelas completas
que se juntaban a las latas vacías y oxidadas
de cerveza Victoria, Light, Kerns
y a las cajas vacías de Corn Flake
y en los excusados habían páginas sueltas
de *Time* junto con los retratos de Somoza
que se pegaban en los biombos de las casas pobres.

CEFERINO, THE PEASANT

When the Praetorian Guard arrived
you were sowing
and turning the earth with your calloused hands.
The sun on your back,
thirst in your throat,
thinking up things in the day
to tell them at night.
When the guard arrived
and asked for your son
you hugged the gourd
and thought of the food hanging from a branch
as if it was meant for a long voyage.
They forced you face down against the earth
and with a rifle, brought you eye to eye with death
(the one John C. Garand invented).
You said nothing
but the trembling of your knees
                              in May
made those of the Guard shake in July
when what you had sown
began to bloom.

———————————

Grethel Cruz
Student
14 years old
Poetry Workshop of Ciudad Dario

CEFERINO, EL CAMPESINO

Cuando llegó la Guardia Pretoriana
estabas sembrando
y con tus manos ásperas trabajabas la tierra.
El sol en la espalda,
con sed en la garganta
pensando cosas en el día
para contarles en la noche.
Cuando llegó la guardia
y preguntaron por tu hijo
abrazaste el calabazo
y pensaste en la comida colgada de un jocote
como para un largo viaje.
Te acostaron como besando la tierra
y te mostraron la muerte apuntándote con un fusil
(el que inventó John C. Garand).
Vos no dijiste nada
pero el temblor de tus rodillas
                              en mayo
hizo trepidar las de los guardias en julio
cuando lo que sembraste
estaba floreciendo.

I WANTED TO MEET YOU

You'll remember, Ernesto Cardenal,
the clandestine trips you made to San Jose.
You must remember
that safe house that belonged to "Eli Moreno."
I'm sure you remember.
You would arrive at midnight.
I wanted to meet you and I woke up the night you arrived
with Jose Valdivia and Eli Moreno.
I spied on you
through the knotholes of my bedroom door.
You spoke serenely of the advances on the Southern Front.
My eyes would fill with tears as I listened to you.
You don't remember me. But I remember you
drinking a cup of coffee
with your black beret over your flowing white hair.

Isabel Romero
Student
Poetry Workshop of Ciudad Sandino

QUERIA CONOCERTE

Te acordarás Ernesto
de los viajes clandestinos que hacías a San José.
Debés de acordarte
de aquella casa de seguridad del compa "Elí Moreno."
Estoy segura que te acordás.
Llegabas a media noche.
Yo quería conocerte y me desperté esa noche que llegaste
con José Valdivia y Elí Moreno.
Los espiaba
por las rendijas de la puerta de mi cuarto,
hablabas sereno de todos los avances en el Frente Sur.
Se me llenaban los ojos de lágrimas al oírte.
Vos no te acordás de mí. Yo sí te recuerdo
tomándote una taza de café
con tu boina negra en tu cabellera blanca.

BICKAR MUNOZ

When I pass by the "Chamorro Industrial" factory
I remember when we were on the inside, liberating the money,
pushing back the security guards,
tying their hands,
the search for the cash,
the slogans I spray-painted on the wall,
the M-3 in your trusted hands,
your poise,
your determined voice shouting:
                    Nobody move—we're from the FSLN!
Everything became hushed.
We did it for our people,
for the workers who made those machines run.
Bickar,
that was how we carried out the operation called
"Workers and Peasants to Power."

Francisco Orozco
People's Sandinista Army
Poetry Workshop of the Third Military Region

BICKAR MUNOZ

Cuando paso a la orilla de la fábrica CHAMORRO INDUSTRIAL
y cuando estuvimos dentro en aquella recuperación de dinero
y los empujones a los celadores
el amarre
la búsqueda de dinero
las pintas que puse en las paredes
la M-3 en tus manos confiadas
la serenidad
tu firmeza al momento de gritar:
                    Nadie se mueva somos del FSLN.
Todo fue silencio.
Lo hacíamos por nuestro pueblo
por esos obreros que manejaban las máquinas.
Bickar,
así se hizo el operativo que llamamos
Obreros y Campesinos al Poder.

THE SCARE

When I was ten, I remember that
my mom, Petrona, was reading
and I was cooking some noodles.
I looked out towards the patio
and thought I saw two turtles,
but they were really the helmets of Somoza's Guard,
then they went around to the back.
                        I got scared
because they looked at me with malice in their eyes.
They told me to open the door and when they came in
I went over by my mom.
"Where are the bastards?" they asked her.
(My brother Alfredo
was trembling for us
in a house across the street
because he was a guerilla fighter.)
She told them she didn't know.
Half an hour later
the bullets began flying by the San Judas Church,
it was May of 1979.

Ileana Larios
12 years old
Poetry Workshop of San Judas

EL SUSTO

Cuando tenía diez años, me acuerdo que
mi mamá Petrona estaba leyendo
y yo cocinando unos tallarines;
miré hacia el patio
y me pareció que habían dos tortugas
pero eran los cascos de los guardias,
después los tuve atrás.
                    Me asusté
porque me miraron con ojos maliciosos.
Me dijeron que abriera la puerta
y cuando entraron
me fui donde mi mamá.
Le preguntaron—¿Dónde están los arrastrados?
—Mi hermano Alfredo
desde otra casa miraba con temor
que nos hicieran algo
porque era guerrillero—.
Ella dijo que no sabía.
Después a la media hora
una fuerte balacera por la iglesia de San Judas,
era mayo de 1979.

54

ANDREA

I still can't accept your death.
I feel sad and alone with your memory.
Yet coming home and finding our daughter
gives me the courage to go on.
I want to see her grow beautiful and honest like you,
full of song and revolution,
as when you stood waving the red and black flag,
crying out the slogans of the people.

———————————————————

Roberto Vargas
People's Sandinista Army
Poetry Workshop of the German Pomares Batallion

JUAN ERRE

It was the 8th of June when you fell
at the side of a barricade.
I only remember the position of your body,
your face torn by a grenade.
I only remember staring at you.
I went towards you and I wept and wept and wept.
I picked up your rifle
and carried on.

———————————————

Xiomara Espinoza
Sandinista Air Force
Poetry Workshop of the Sandinista Air Force

ANDREA

No logro creer que estés muerta.
Me siento solo y triste con tu recuerdo.
Llegar a casa y encontrar a nuestra hija
me anima a seguir.
Verla crecer linda y honesta como vos
llena de canto y revolución
como cuando agitabas la bandera rojinegra y gritabas
consignas para el triunfo.

JUAN ERRE

Era un 8 de junio cuando vos caíste muerto
a la orilla de una barricada.
Sólo recuerdo como quedó tu cuerpo
tu cara charneleada.
Sólo recuerdo cuando te miré.
Me acerqué a vos y lloré, lloré, lloré.
Agarré tu fusil
y seguí de frente.

ROUTINE

I watch the leaves falling from the trees,
whirled over the green fields
by the persistent wind.
In solitude,
sitting amid the tall grass
I spoke intimately to myself.
In solitude
I have sought companionship.
In solitude
I have sought love.

———————————

Socorro Peralta
Paralyzed in combat during the insurrection
Poetry Workshop of the Gaspar Garcia Laviana Rehabilitation Center

IT DOESN'T MATTER
(To my comrades injured in battle)

It doesn't matter
that Mario Peralta's fingers were twisted into a claw
by that Guardman's bullet.
Mario,
paralyzed in combat,
                              is in a wheelchair now.
It doesn't matter that my left leg is withering
from that fracture in the spine . . .
We made the Revolution.
We're going to defend it as we are.

———————————————

Alberto Garcia
Sandinista Police
Poetry Workshop of the Ajax Delgado Central Headquarters

RUTINA

Veo caer las hojas de los árboles
que el viento tenaz arremolina
sobre los verdes prados.
Sola
sentada sobre el zacate
hablaba íntimamente.
Sola
he buscado compañía.
Sola
he buscado un amor.

NO IMPORTA
(A mis compañeros lisiados de guerra)

No importa
que Mario Peralta tenga los dedos gafos
por la bala que le disparó un guardia nacional.
Mario
el que quedó inhabilitado después del combate
                              ahora está en silla de ruedas.
No importa que a mí se me seque la pierna izquierda
por la fractura en la columna vertebral.
Nosotros hicimos la Revolución
y asi vamos a defenderla.

58

YOUR EYES

I barely remember your body.
In these years of not seeing you
you must have changed quite a lot.
I imagine your breasts now that you're a woman,
your legs longer, rounder,
                more beautiful—
yet something must be left from that young figure.
This afternoon
              the sky
seems to have the same color as your eyes,
your blue eyes
alive
      like sunflowers at morning.
That must be the only thing which has not changed
from that body I once knew.

THE NIGHT OF THE MEETING

The night of the First National Meeting of the Poetry Workshops
there was a celebration.
While I was dancing I heard
a poet
say to his comrade:
"I always wanted to touch you this way."

Manuel Matute
Factory worker
Militia volunteer
Poetry Workshop of Palacaguina

TUS OJOS

Apenas recuerdo tu cuerpo.
En estos años sin verte
ya habrás cambiado mucho.
Imagino tus senos desarrollados
tus piernas largas redondas
                        más bellas
algo habrá quedado de aquella figura.
Esta tarde
          el cielo
me parece que tiene el mismo color de tus ojos
tus ojos azules
vivos
        como girasoles en la mañana.
Esto debe ser lo único que no ha cambiado
de aquel cuerpo.

LA NOCHE DEL ENCUENTRO

La noche del Encuentro Nacional de los Talleres de Poesía
hubo fiesta.
Mientras bailaba oí
que un poeta
decía a su compañera:
—Siempre había querido tocarte así.

WHEN YOU DISCOVER

When you read the poems I've written about you
you'll feel proud.
But what will you say when you discover
that I wrote them as a simple reference
to the past,
and that today
the one to whom I give my kisses and more
is Rogelio
the Sandinista.

THE VIRGIN MARY

When I'm on the beach and see
the shapely legs of Marina, my friend,
I wonder: Are Mary's legs that way?
If I see the beautiful eyes of my niece, Johanna,
I wonder: Are Mary's eyes that way?
When I see the statuesque body
of a young woman I don't know, I wonder:
Is Mary's body that way?
When I gaze at my naked breasts and with the palm
of my hand trace their shape, I wonder:
Are Mary's breasts this way?

Cony Pacheco
Nurse
Poetry Workshop of Subtiava

CUANDO SEPAS

Cuando leás los poemas que he escrito para vos
te sentirás orgulloso.
Pero qué dirás cuando sepás
que los escribí para hacer referencia
de un pasado,
y que hoy
a quien doy mis besos y más
es a Rogelio
el sandinista.

ASI ES MARIA

Cuando en la playa miro
las torneadas piernas de Marina, mi amiga,
pienso: ¿Serán así las piernas de María?.
Si veo los bellos ojos de mi sobrina, la Johanna,
pienso: ¿Así serán los ojos de María?.
Al ver el bien delineado cuerpo
de una chica desconocida, pienso:
¿Será así el cuerpo de María?.
Cuando veo mis senos desnudos y con la palma
de la mano recorro su contorno me pregunto:
¿Así serán los senos de María?

THE DANCE OF THE PALM

When your first son died,
compadre Emilio built the coffin
and Dona Pura gathered the palm branches.
At the wake,
on a small table, the coffin and the palm branches,
the lamp to one side.
The neighbors were seated on some benches.
You wept, Maria.
Don Ciriaco and his sons
with their guitars and accordions
played the Dance of the Palm for the dead child.
The couples danced solemnly
before the small coffin.

Julia Aguirre
Occupation unavailable
Poetry Workshop of Palacaguina

EL BAILE DE LA PALMA

Cuando murió tu primer hijo
el compadre Emilio hizo el ataúd
y doña Pura las palmas.
En la vela
en una mesa pequeña el ataúd y las palmas,
a un lado el candil.
Los vecinos sentados en unos bancos.
Vos llorabas, María.
Don Ciriaco y sus hijos
con guitarras y bandolinas
le hicieron el baile de la palma al niño muerto.
Las parejas bailaron
frente al ataúd pequeño.

DARLING

Every time I see you walking
to Dona Chepita's grocery store
I get the urge to walk with you.
Thinking of doing that makes me nervous.
How I'd love to put my arms around you,
tell you that I love you!
Being ten years old, thinking of doing that
makes me nervous.

———————————

Abbey Melec Alvarado
Campesino
Poetry Workshop of Niquinohomo

COMPANERO UMANZOR

During breakfast in my office
at the Ministry of the Interior,
you asked me: "Have you finished?"
And you cleaned up the plates on which I had eaten.
You are an officer and my superior,
and your gesture could only come from a Sandinista.

———————————

Mario Bolanos
Sandinista Police
Poetry Workshop of the Ministry of the Interior

DARLING

Siempre que te veo pasar
a la pulpería de doña Chepita
me dan ganas de acompañarte.
Pensar en hacerlo me provocan nervios.
Cómo me gustaría abrazarte
decirte que te quiero.
A mis diez años pensar en hacerlo
me provocan nervios.

COMPANERO UMANZOR

Cuando desayunábamos en mi oficina
del Ministerio del Interior,
me dijiste: ¿ya terminaste?
y te fuiste con los platos donde había comido yo.
Vos sos Oficial y mi Superior,
y tu gesto sólo lo puede tener un sandinista

I WONDER

I wonder
at the life of a man
who is not loved.
It must be like the silence at dawn,
or the Masaya Lagoon,
stagnant and serene,
where the sun's reflection is like a fish
that leaps at noon . . .
or it must be
like a foreigner who has just arrived.

Carlos Pacheco
Occupation unavailable
Poetry Workshop of Masaya

YO ME PREGUNTO

Yo me pregunto
cómo es la vida de un hombre
que no es amado.
Debe ser como el silencio en la madrugada
o como la Laguna de Masaya
estancada y serena
donde el reflejo del sol es como un pez
que aletea al medio día
o debe ser
como un extranjero recién llegado.

VIGILANCE

With their cry
the roosters seem to be reaching for dawn.
The sun is not yet up.
I see the dark shadows
of the sentries near the trench
moving carefully.
Now the dawn is here:
The sound of the corn in the mill,
the rustling of the birds in the trees,
a fresh fragrance brought by the wind.
The thick whiteness of the fog
slowly lifts and reveals the hills.
The sun.
A new morning,
and at my feet, a lake, clear as a mirror.

Francisco Arteaga
Occupation unavailable
Poetry Workshop of Ocotal

VIGILANCIA

Con el canto
los gallos parcen buscar la madrugada.
Aún no amanece.
Miro la sombra oscura
de los postas junto a la trinchera
                    moviéndose cuidadosamente.
Ahora contemplo la madrugada:
el ruido del molino,
el aleteo de los pájaros en los árboles,
una fragancia fresca que trae el viento.
La blancura espesa de la neblina
poco a poco despeja los cerros.
El sol.
Una mañana nueva,
y a mis pies una laguna clara como un espejo.

OVER THE GRAVE OF LAUREANO

Laureano: I soar over your grave in a plane
staring at the foam on the lake
and see the white stones circling your tomb . . .
It occurs to me that this plane could plummet from the sky
and in minutes the circle of white foam would vanish forever.

Alejandro Guevara
People's Sandinista Army
Poetry Workshop of the First Military Region

UPON THE STONE

The strong winds of January and February
have stilled. And now the calm weather
of March and April is arriving.
The river has dried up where the huge stone was,
all engraved with hieroglyphs,
seemingly motionless . . .
Yet it moves,
because the earth moves and the stone is upon the earth.
The importance of the stone
is that upon it, one afternoon, you and I kissed,
Maria Olimpia.

Ivan Guevara
People's Sandinista Army
Poetry Workshop of the Camilo Ortega Saavedra Batallion

SOBRE LA TUMBA DE LAUREANO

Laureano: paso en avión sobre tu tumba
y he estado viendo las espumas del lago
y veo el círculo de piedras blanqueadas de tu tumba,
pienso que podría caer en este avión
y a los minutos el círculo de espuma blanca desaparecería.

SOBRE LA PIEDRA

Han dejado de soplar los vientos fuertes
de enero y febrero. Y ahora viene el tiempo calmo
de marzo y abril.
Se ha secado el río, donde estaba la inmensa piedra
grabada toda con jeroglíficos
estática aparentemente;
sin embargo se mueve
porque la tierra se mueve y la piedra está sobre la tierra.
La importancia que tiene la piedra
es que en ella una tarde nos besamos
María Olimpia.

MEMORY

Standing
at the edge of Masaya Lake
on the evening of the 14th of November
we made love
and on my clothes a small stain of blood remained.
Days later, as a gift, you gave me a handkerchief
clean clean clean
white.

———

Gerardo Gadea
People's Sandinista Army
Poetry Workshop of Moimbo

SANDINO

I imagine Sandino and Blanca Arauz
in the mountains
or on a bench, speaking in quiet voices
about the guerilla struggle
and secretly thinking corny things
about each other.

————

Javier Ortiz
11 years old
Newspaper boy
Poetry Workshop of Monimbo

RECUERDO

De pie
a orillas de la Laguna de Masaya
la tarde del 14 de noviembre
hicimos el amor
y en la ropa me quedó una manchita de sangre.
Días después me entregaste el pañuelo
limpio limpio limpio
blanco.

SANDINO

Yo imagino a Sandino y a Blanca Araúz
sentados los dos en la montaña
o en un banco platicando
de la guerrilla
y pensando cosas sentimentales
de ellos dos.

AN ORDER

In the secret office, three of us rested
on wooden crates,
Carlos lying on a damp and dirty mattress
with green and pink stripes
covered with hair (it had been in the barber shop).
Two pieces of newspaper as a sheet
and an M-25 at his side.
I was on a large wooden table
and could not sleep,
remembering the smile of my child
after his milk in the morning.
We were re-assigned to the Anti-Air Defense Command.
Everyone seemed asleep
with their uniforms and boots on
and weapons at their sides. Many hours had passed.
I got up
as the rays of the sun
pierced the dawn like spears.

Ana Sofia Martinez
Sandinista Air Force
Poetry Workshop of the Sandinista Air Force

UNA ORDEN

En la Oficina Secreta, reposábamos tres personas,
sobre cajones de madera,
Carlos acostado sobre un colchón rayado
en verde y rosado, sucio, húmedo
lleno de pelo (antes estaba en la barbería),
tenía por sobrecama dos pliegos de periódicos
a su lado una M-25.
Yo sobre una mesa grande de madera
no podía conciliar el sueño,
recordando la sonrisa de mi hijo
después de tomarse su leche en la mañana.
Estábamos reconcentrados en la FAS-DAA.
Todos están aparentemente dormidos
con el uniforme y las botas puestas
y nuestras armas al lado. Han pasado muchas horas.
Me levanto
mientras los rayos del sol
atraviesan la penumbra como lanzas.

76

POEM TO A NEIGHBORHOOD ORGANIZER

It was on a winter night
that we knew each other
                    intimately.
You asked me if I was cold.
At that moment
I felt you edging closer and closer to my bed.
Your nearness quickened my heart.
Your body
began to join mine
until we became one single body.
For which I am not sorry.

Lesbia Rodriguez
Occupation unavailable
Poetry Workshop of Bello Horizonte

AT THE RIVER

At the Tamarindo River I found him.
While I bathed his eyes
fell upon me.
He invited me to his home
and I went barefoot on a narrow path
of stones.
The startled chickens scattered
and the hummingbirds darted from branch to branch
filling their mouths with honey.

Juana Maria Huete
Domestic employee
Literacy teacher
Poetry Workshop of Subtiava

POEMA A UN CEDECISTA

Fue una noche de invierno
que nos conocimos
                    íntimamente.
Me preguntaste si sentía frío.
En ese momento
sentí acercarte poco a poco a mi cama.
Tu cercanía aceleró mi corazón.
Tu cuerpo
se fue juntando al mío
hasta quedar en un solo cuerpo.
De lo que no me arrepiento.

EN EL RIO

En el Río Tamarindo lo encontré.
Mientras me bañaba dirigía
la vista hacia mí.
Me invitó a su casa
y fui descalza por un camino angosto
de piedras.
Las gallinas se asustaron
y los gorriones saltaban de una rama a otra
chupando miel.

78

ON THE PATHS OF NIQUINOHOMO

I love the paths of Niquinohomo:
El Guapinol, Tierra Blanca, La Hoja Chigue.
The paths lined with cedars, guachipilines and guanacastes,
that smell of earth in winter,
where women pass by, vessels of water on their heads,
on foot or mule-back,
leaving a trail behind.
They make me think of the birds
that soar above those paths.

Miguel Quijano Macanche
Campesino
Militia volunteer
15 years of age
Poetry Workshop of Niquinohomo

EGRETS

Sitting on the slope of a ravine
I saw a flock of white egrets
alight, their legs long and thin
like wooden stakes.
I stood up
and walked towards them.
Not to be touched, they rose in flight.
In the immense sky they were like pieces of cotton
                              pulled along by the wind.

Juan Bautista Paiz
Campesino
Militia volunteer
Learned to read and write during Literacy Campaign of 1980
Poetry Workshop of San Sebastian

EN LOS CAMINOS DE NIQUINOHOMO

Me gustan los caminos de Niquinohomo:
El Guapinol, Tierra Blanca, La Hoja Chigüe.
Los caminos que tienen cedros, guachipilines y guanacastes
los que huelen a tierra en invierno
donde pasan las mujeres acarreando su cántaro de agua
a pie o a caballo
y van dejando rastro.
Me parecen como los pájaros
que vuelan por esos caminos.

GARZAS

Sentado en la ladera de un barranco
miré posarse cerca
una parvada de garzas patonas
larguchas como estacas.
Me puse de pie
avancé hacia ellas.
Ariscas se suspendieron en vuelo.
En el inmenso cielo parecían algodón desmotado
                                    arrastrado por el viento.

TO THE COMBATANT JUAN BUSTAMANTE
OF THE SOUTHERN FRONT

It was six in the evening, on the 17th of February, 1980
when I fell in love with you, Juan.
You were wearing your camouflage uniform,
a rifle on the desk,
carrying out your twenty four hours of sentry duty.
I went up to you
and touched your dark brown skin.

Nidia Taylor Ellis
People's Sandinista Army
Poetry Workshop of El Bluff (Bluefields)

DOUBT OF LOVE

You've become accustomed to my way
to such an extent
that when I say, "Love,
the Revolution requires
                    that I go away for some time,"
you answer:
                    "I understand clearly, comrade."
And it's then when I start to feel
a twinge of doubt about our love.

Isidoro Tercero
Sandinista Police
Poetry Workshop of the State Security Division

AL COMBATIENTE JUAN BUSTAMANTE DEL FRENTE SUR

Eran las seis de la tarde del día 17 de febrero de 1980
cuando de vos me enamoré, Juan.
Con tu uniforme de camuflaje
y tu GALIL encima del escritorio
cumpliendo tus veinticuatro horas de posta
me acerqué a vos
y toqué tu piel color de chocolate..

CIERTA DUDA DE AMOR

Te acostumbraste a mi forma de ser
de tal manera
que cuando te digo, amor,
que la Revolución necesita de nosotros
                                que me marche
vos me contestás:
                —Estoy de acuerdo, camarada.
Y es entonces cuando siento
cierta duda de nuestro amor.

MILITIA WOMAN

I had dreamt about you.
Between my hands,
a rose, a lily
and a captured bird.
I was among wild grasses,
jack-rabbits, owls,
seagulls and sparrows.
I began to walk . . .
I saw you
with your olive green uniform and the jacket
you wore when I met you, militia woman.
In the long corridor
a cat,
a fishing net hanging from an oar,
and a bunch of pijibay fruit
the color of your trousers.
I freed the bird
and walked towards you.
The lily and the rose
I placed in your hand
were to say
    that I love you, militia woman.

John Taylor
Fishing fleet mechanic
Poetry Workshop of Bluefields

MILICIANA

Había soñado con vos.
Entre mis manos,
una rosa, un lirio
y un pájaro preso.
Entre pastos
conejos, búhos
gaviotas y golondrinas.
Caminé
miré en vos
ese verde olivo y la chaqueta
con que te conocí miliciana.
En el corredor
un gato,
una atarralla cuelga de un remo
y un gajo de pijibay
color de tu pantalón.
Liberé al pájaro
y fui en busca de vos.
El lirio y la rosa
que deposité en tu mano
fueron como decirte
                    te quiero miliciana.

TRINOMIOS

My intention was to write you a poem
that would say that as a woman and as a lover
you had burrowed deep into my emotions.
Because of you
the barking of the dogs at midnight
doesn't bother me.
Nor do I stumble out to the dark patio
to throw sticks, shoes, stones or whatever
when the passionate cats
raise hell on the zinc roof.
Also, I hardly ever think of death.

Six intervening elements
don't allow me to conclude
what I had originally intended:
Eisenhower less than Johnson,
Begin more than Roosevelt,
Taft less than Reagan.

These are visions that awaken feelings
in those of us
who were, or are, predestined to feel.
I have seen many women weeping,
and also a man, at the edge of the Coco River.*

Eisenhower more than Roosevelt and less than Johnson
Begin more than Taft and less than Reagan.
Nevertheless, my intention was to write you a poem.

Manuel Mena
Construction worker
Poetry Workshop of Colonia 14 de Septiembre
*Coco River – common border of Nicaragua and Honduras

TRINOMIOS

Mi intención era hacerte un poema
que dijera que como mujer y como amante
habías penetrado en mis sentimientos.
Con vos
los ladridos de los perros a media noche
no me causan molestia,
ni salgo al patio oscuro
a lanzar palos, zapatos, piedras o lo que sea
cuando los gatos enamorados
arman alboroto en el techo de zinc.
Además casi ni pienso en la muerte.
Seis elementos interferentes
no me dejan terminar
lo que al principio quise hacer:
Eisenhower menos que Johnson,
Begin más que Roosevelt
Taft menos que Reagan.
Son visiones que despiertan sentimientos
de aquellos que estaban o estábamos
predestinados a sentir siempre.
Yo he visto a muchas mujeres llorando;
también a un hombre en la margen del Río Coco.
Eisenhower más que Roosevelt y menos que Johnson
Begin más que Taft y menos que Reagan.
Y sin embargo mi intención era hacerte un poema.

MADHOUSE
(I Imagine New York)

The mad are like answers no one has asked for.
They're like the spokes of a wagon wheel with no hub,
like rain beating from the ground up,
like test pilots stuck in bluish mud.
The city breathes through the lungs of its mad,
dresses in suits tailored by its mad,
rides in the cars driven by its mad,
orders, obeys,
and cheats through its mad.
The lawyer designs houses and the witchdoctor chants mass,
the teacher sells fish and the stretcherbearer lectures the scholars.
A more powerful madness would be
                    needed to finish with this madhouse.

Antonio Campbell
Law student
Poetry Workshop of Bluefields

MANICOMIO
(Imagino a New York)

Los locos son como respuestas que nadie ha pedido.
Son como los rayos de una carreta sin eje,
como una lluvia que azota de abajo hacia arriba,
como pilotos de prueba atascados en el barro celeste.
La ciudad respira por los pulmones de sus locos,
se viste con traje que cortaron sus locos,
va en los autómoviles que conducen sus locos;
ordena, obedece,
y hace trampa a través de sus locos.
El abogado diseña las casas y el hechicero canta la misa,
el maestro vende pescado y el camillero sirve las cátedras.
Se necesitaría una locura mayor para acabar con este manicomio.

E CORTES TREE

n Santa Teresa of Carazo
nature created a beautiful cortes tree.
Its wide shade was a delight to everyone's eyes.
But life was a fleeting thing;
with hatchets and machetes they took the tree.
They deprived us of her presence;
for money they took from us
the shadows of her yellow flowers.

Ana Leonor Cruz
Textile worker
Learned to read and write in 1980 Literacy Campaign
Poetry Workshop of the Sandinista Workers Federation

EL CORTES

En Santa Teresa de Carazo
la naturaleza creó un hermoso árbol de cortés.
Su gran sombra era un deleite a la vista de todos.
Pero la vida duró poco,
se la quitaron con hacha y machete.
Nos privaron de su presencia,
por dinero nos quitaron
su sombra de flores amarillas.

IN JINOTEGA

The sun rises over the Hill of Love,
over Yacapuca, La Tejera, Mancotal and Apanas.
The children come down from the hills,
the mothers, grandparents and fathers,
to the Health Clinic and the Amin Halum Hospital.
Nicasio and Bacilizo with diarrhea, cough,
ulcers and open sores on their feet.
Josefa Palacios comes in shivering
and I begin to unwrap two, three, six rags,
a dirty bathrobe and pants beneath.
She is pregnant and hasn't bathed
in eight months out of superstition.
She is covered with fleas.
Others come with fungus infections,
                                    tuberculosis,
heads swollen with pus
(pus of staphylococcus, pus of streptococcus),
mountain leprosy around the eyes.
I wait for night to fall.
A wounded companero arrives,
the same young man I treated at the Eduardo Contreras School
when I was in charge of the Military Health Unit.
I lie down and my mind wanders:
I remember the voice of the old woman from Los Planes de Vilan,
the lady of Tomatoya,
the smiles, the thanks
                        and the weeping.
And the emergency calls go on,
on Sunday at 11 p.m.
                        at 2, at 5 in the morning
(my constant weariness and nervousness)
That's the way it is in Wiwili,
La Rica, Raiti, Bocay.
And I know soon all will change with the Revolution.

Juan Herrera
Intern
Poetry Workshop of Jinotega

EN JINOTEGA

Sale el sol por la Cuesta del Amor,
por Yucapuca, La Tejera, Mancotal y Apanás.
Bajan los niños, las mamás, los abuelos
los hombres
al Centro de Salud y al Hospital Amín Halum.
Nicasio, Bacilizo con diarrea, con tos,
con úlcera y los pies hediondos.
Llega la Josefa Palacios
y empiezo a quitar dos, tres, seis trapos,
una bata debajo y un pantalón.
Un gran frío y ocho meses de no bañarse
por estar embarazada.
Toda llena de piojos.
Otros vienen con hongos
con tuberculosis
con la cabeza llena de pus
(pus de estafilococos, pus de estreptococos)
y con lepra de montaña cerca de los ojos.
Espero la noche.
Llega un compa herido
el mismo que atendí en la Escuela Eduardo Contreras
en mi control de Sanidad Militar.
Me acuesto y comienzo a recordar:
recuerdo la voz de la vieja de Los Planes de Vilán,
la señora de Tomatoya,
las sonrisas, las gracias
y los llantos.
Y continúan las llamadas de emergencia
del domingo a las once de la noche
a las dos, a las cinco
(yo solo cansado y nervioso).
Así sucede en Wiwilí,
La Rica, Raití, Bocay.
Y sé que pronto todo cambiará con la Revolución.

LOVE BETWEEN RESERVISTS

Mariel
let me begin to kiss your face,
your lips,
your body.
Perhaps tomorrow it will be too late
and the Yankee Marines will be here again.
Then you and I will no longer be together.
You'll be healing the wounded companeros
behind the lines,
and I'll be in the line of fire.

Juan Ignacio Centeno
Member of the Sandinista Youth Organization
Poetry Workshop of Condega

AMOR ENTRE RESERVISTAS

Mariel
déjame que ahora empiece a besar tus mejillas
tus labios
tu cuerpo.
Quizá mañana sea tarde
y estén aquí de nuevo los de la Marina Yanqui.
Entonces vos y yo ya no estaremos juntos.
Vos estarás en la reserva médica a la retaguardia
curando los compañeros heridos
y yo en la línea de fuego.

IT'S TWELVE, THIRTEEN SECONDS INTO DAWN

From the cramped space where I sleep
I can see the black trunk of a tree in the field,
strands of barbed wire, pieces of cardboard,
and the moon, which seems to strip itself of the dark clouds

and its light emerges
like a political prisoner brought up
from the cramped, filthy cells.
The motor of a truck is heard in the distance
on the Acoyapa or Rama road

> (Heard faintly on Radio Havana:
> "I will keep a final resting place
> for you on earth.")*

The dogs bark, one, then another, then others.
Roosters crow nearby.
It dawns.

————————

Julio Madrigal
Occupation unavailable
Poetry Workshop of Chontales
*cp. *John* 14: 1–3.

SON LAS DOCE, TRECE SEGUNDOS DE LA MADRUGADA

En el lugar estrecho donde duermo
se mira al fondo un palo madero negro,
hilos de alambre de púas, pedazos de cartón,
y miro la luna que parece desnudarse de las negras nubes

y sale su luz
como cuando sacan un preso político
de los cuartos estrechos y hediondos.
Se oye la máquina de un furgón que pasa lejos
sobre la carretera Acoyapa o Rama
           (En Radio Habana se escucha bajito:
           te guardaré un lugar en la tierra
           para morir).
Los perros ladran uno, otro, otros
Los gallos cantan cerca.
Amanece.

ON DEFENSE

And there are revolutions
like the one in Chile
with Salvador Allende
who left his people unarmed
in the days of the Popular Unity Government.
And falling once again into exploiting hands
the peasants and workers
were divided, marginalized.
That's why in Nicaragua
there are batallions of women
of students
of peasants
of workers
the whole people prepared for defense.

Jorge Vega
People's Sandinista Army
Poetry Workshop of El Bluff (Bluefields)

EN LA DEFENSA

Y hay Revoluciones
como la de Chile
con Salvador Allende
que no armó a su pueblo
en los días del triunfo de la Unidad Popular
y los obreros y trabajadores
apartados, marginados
cuando cayeron de nuevo en manos explotadoras.
Por eso en Nicaragua
existen batallones de muchachas
de estudiantes
de campesinos
de obreros,
el pueblo dispuesto a la defensa.

ARRIVALS

Aided and financed by Isabela, Queen of Spain,
Christopher Columbus arrived in America
with three sailing ships:
                    The Pinta, the Nina and the Santa Maria.
He had set off hoping to find the Indies,
but lost, arrived in Guarani (now called the Bahamas).
He usurped the indigenous name,
                    and christened the land "San Salvador."
His men raped, brought venereal disease, horses
and weapons to massacre the Indians
(all of them were white men).
Now to another San Salvador, marines arrive
bringing mortars, helicopters and jet planes
to massacre the Salvadorean people,
and they are aided
and financed by the multinational monopolies,
                                        by Imperialism.

Benjamin Monge
Literacy teacher
Electrical engineering student
Poetry Workshop of Colonia 14 de Septiembre

LLEGADAS

Ayudado y financiado por la reina Isabel de España
Cristóbal Colón llegó a América
con tres carabelas:
                    La Pinta, la Niña y la Santa María.
Navegó buscando las Indias
y extraviado llegó a Guaraní (hoy las Bahamas).
Usurpó el nombre indígena
                    y le llamó San Salvador.
Violaron, trajeron enfermedades venéreas, caballos
y armas para asesinar indios
(eran todos europeos).
Ahora en otro San Salvador llegan marines
que traen obuses, helicópteros, aviones
para asesinar a la población salvadoreña,
y son ayudados
y financiados por las transnacionales,
                    el imperialismo.

VISION OF THE FUTURE THROUGH A KISS

When our lips unite
it's like a historical process accelerates inside me.
I imagine healthy children
playing freely in the parks of the world
studying in children's libraries.
Parents and children working together.
Lovers talking about love, planning their studies and careers,
agricultural workers on tractors built by themselves
plowing huge fields to be sown.
During the rainy season, the earth
                            like an immense green tennis ball,
preventive medicine for all.
Only traffic police
(no need for any other kind)
no armies or war machines.
The earth without political maniacs or sexual ones
robbery like a memory in the history texts.
No multinational monopolies.
The earth a single nation
and what are now countries
will be like states in the new world
a single world anthem for all
gigantic granaries and power plants like cities
bookstores without pornography or alienating soap opera mags
Cosmopolitan, magazine of the World Department of Education
shall inform of breakthroughs
then those who were the owners of the means of production
shall be ashamed to admit it
it will be like speaking about prostitution
or mass murder
money won't be needed
a single human family
without distinctions or class or race
equality for all
love given in return for love.
Everyone working to live and living for everyone.

VISION DEL FUTURO A TRAVES DE UN BESO

Unir nuestros labios
es como acelerar un proceso histórico dentro de mí.
Imagino niños sanos
jugando libres en los parques del mundo
estudiando en bibliotecas infantiles.
Padres e hijos trabajando juntos.
Parejas de enamorados
en pláticas de amor planean el estudio y el trabajo,
trabajadores agrícolas en tractores fabricados por ellos
preparan inmensos campos para cultivarlos.
En invierno, la tierra como una inmensa pelota de tenis verde,
medicinia preventiva para todos.
Policías de tránsito solamente
(no habrá necesidad de otros),
sin ejércitos, ni máquinas de guerra.
La tierra sin maniáticos políticos y sexuales
los robos como un recuerdo en los textos de historia.
Sin transnacionales.
El mundo una sola nación
los que ahora son países
serán como departamentos en este nuevo mundo
un solo himno mundial para todos
gigantes graneros y plantas eléctricas como ciudades
librerías sin literaturas pornográficas y fotonovelas alienantes
Cosmopólitan del Ministerio mundial de Educación
informará sobre los avances
entonces aquellos que fueron dueños de los medios de producción
sentirán vergüenza de decirlo
será como hablar de prostitución
o de un asesinato colectivo
no será necesario el dinero
un solo género humano
sin distingo de clase, ni de raza
igualdad de derechos para todos
amor igual a amor.
Todos trabajando para vivir y viviendo para todos.

Giant billboards along the roads
announcing conferences about love, scientific ones, cultural ones
everything is solidarity in this vision
union
like the union of our lips
it's like feeling now
the beginning of a new life.

Benjamin Monge
Poetry Workshop of Colonia 14 de Septiembre

Gigantes afiches en las calles
anuncian encuentros de amor, científicos y culturales
todo es solidaridad en este pensamiento

                              unión

como la unión de nuestros labios,
es como sentir ahora
el principio de una nueva vida.

I HAD HEARD ABOUT YOU

I had heard about you
but in a Cuban magazine I got to know you better.
You were an old guy, nearly bald,
and I learned that you were a painter of life
from beginning to end.
And the rumor around Paris
was that you did it all in your underwear.
And the passion you had for women
you also had for your homeland.
When Somoza bombed Leon, Masaya and Esteli
with Yankee planes and bombs,
Franco had already bombed Guernica
with Fascist planes and bombs.
I'm dedicating this poem to you,
a sweet old guy named Picasso.

Oscar Alonso
Carpenter
Militia volunteer
Poetry Workshop of Colonia Centro America

HABIA OIDO DE VOS

Había oído de vos
pero en una revista cubana te conocí más.
Eras un viejo casi pelón
y supe que fuiste pintor de la vida
de principio a fin;
y la chismería de París
decía que lo hacías en calzoncillo.
Así como amaste mujeres
amaste tu patria.
Cuando Somoza bombardeó León, Masaya y Estelí
con aviones y bombas yankis
Franco ya había bombardeado Guernica
con aviones y bombas hitlerianas.
Este poema te lo dedico a vos
que eras un viejo llamado Picasso.

HERE ON THE BORDER

The Negro River
where we bathe at dawn,
the birds,
the bramble thickets,
the mountain filled with weird sounds,
the ground soaked through by the rain,
and me on sentry duty,
imagining you, Malvina.

MALVINA

I won't write you today
like I used to in the city.
I know tomorrow is Valentine's Day
and we won't be together.
The mountain is as dark as your hair.
The night birds sing
their mysterious songs,
Coffee shells are washed away
by the Blanco River.
My jaw is stiff with the cold.
The butt of my rifle is freezing.
In ambush we wait for the Contra.

Manuel Urtecho
Factory worker
Militia volunteer
Poetry Workshop of FUNDECI Industry Workers

AQUI IN LA FRONTERA

El Río Negro
donde nos bañamos en las madrugadas,
los pájaros
los matorrales de zarzas,
la montaña llena de ruidos extraños,
el suelo mojado a causa de la lluvia
y yo haciendo posta
pensando en vos, Malvina.

MALVINA

Hoy no te escribiré
como en la ciudad.
Sé que mañana será el día de los enamorados
y no estaremos juntos.
La montaña oscura como tu pelo.
Los pájaros nocturnos
con sus cantos misteriosos.
El Río Blanco
arrastrando pulpas de café.
Mi quijada dura por el frío.
La culata de mi fusil helada.
Emboscados esperamos al enemigo.

IN DARIO CITY

The room is small where I write my poems,
where I dream at night
and shelter my memories.
An old, over-stuffed bed,
a dusty mirror
that makes things larger than life,
two wooden suitcases,
a box nailed to the wall
where the medicine is stored,
a black leather bag for my books
and a couple of shirts.
And on a small table
a faint light.
Here I write my poems.

Fernando Rodriguez
Literacy teacher
Militia volunteer
Poetry Workshop of Dario City

EN CIUDAD DARIO

Es pequeño el sitio donde escribo mis poemas
sueño en las noches
y guardo mis recuerdos.
Una cama grande acolchonada y vieja
un espejo polvoso
que agranda las cosas,
dos valijas de madera
un cajón pegado a la pared
donde permanecen las medicinas,
una valija de cuero negro donde guardo mis libros
y algunas camisas.
Y sobre una pequeña mesa
una bujía de noche.
Aquí escribo mis versos.

CARMEN

When you aren't speaking softly in my ear,
it's like I'm living in a world
where all the birds have lost their voices.

FOR JOSE RAMON CORDERO

Jose Ramon,
winter has greened
the high Chontalenan mountains
and the dove coos sadly
as if missing your presence.
The heliotropes and honeysuckle
perfume the paths
you once travelled
and the guardabarranco,
flying overhead, lets fall
precious feathers
onto the place where you fell asleep.

MY LOVE

I'll leave at dawn.
The green mountains with their flowering poplars
will stay behind.
The winds and sun will follow me.
I leave my grayish sky with its perpetual breeze
and its flight of swallows.

Jose Domingo Moreno
Campesino
Learned to read and write in Literacy Campaign of 1980
Poetry Workshop of Jinotega

CARMEN

Cuando no me hablás al oído
me parece vivir en un mundo de pájaros mudos.

A JOSE RAMON CORDERO

José Ramón
ya el invierno reverdeció
las altas montañas yaleñas
y el guas canta triste
como extrañando tu presencia.
Los heliotropos y madreselvas
perfuman los caminos
que vos anduviste
y el guardabarranco
al pasar nos deja caer
preciosas plumas
en el sitio donde te dormiste.

AMOR

Al alba partiré.
Atrás quedarán las verdes montañas
con sus álamos floridos.
el viento y el sol me seguirán.
Dejo mi cielo gris con su perenne brisa
y su vuelo de golondrinas.

AMPARO

I met her one summer.
I had only been there a few days, in that place of dusty streets
and sad afternoons.
She sold fruit-bread at the Somoto bus station.
A number of months passed.
I would ask around for her.
And on the 19th of July I found her amid that great crowd.
I held out my hands and full of emotion we embraced.
It was a fleeting thing.
Someone called her and she climbed into a truck,
and among young men,
I only saw her wave her hand.
She was leaving for the border to stop the enemy aggression.

Jose Domingo Moreno
Poetry Workshop of Jinotega

AMPARO

La conocí un verano.
Yo tenía pocos días de haber llegado a aquel lugar
de calles polvorientas
y de atardeceres tristes.
Ella vendía rosquillas en la *COTRAN* de Somoto.
Pasaron unos meses.
Pregunté por ella
Y el 19 de julio la encontré en medio de la muchedumbre.
Le tendí mis manos y emocionados nos abrazamos.
Aquello fue breve
alguien la llamó y se subió a un camión
y en medio de muchachos
sólo vi que agitó su mano.
Iba rumbo a la frontera a detener al enemigo.

114

FOUR MONTHS

More than four months
without seeing you.
In one week
the malinche in the park
gave thousands of red
                    flowers.
How many kisses would we have given each other
                    in four months.
In Santa Lucia
the cinnamon trees are giving flowers
yellower than last year
and more fragrant
and the sun does not wither them.
The pages of the books
we read together
are yellowing
because you haven't touched them.
In spite of everything
the flowers of the malinche
are fragrant
and red.

Adelaida Diaz
Occupation unavailable
Poetry Workshop of Boaco

4 MESES

Más de cuatro meses
sin verte.
En una semana
el malinche del parque
dio miles de flores
                    rojas.
Cuántos besos nos hubiéramos dado en cuatro meses.
En Santa Lucía
las cañafístolas están dando flores
más amarillas que el año pasado
y más olorosas
y el sol no las marchita.
Las páginas de los libros
que leímos juntos
 se están poniendo amarillentas
porque no las has tocado vos,
a pesar de todo
las flores del malinche
huelen
y son rojas.

NOHEMY

What would I do without
                the warmth of your mouth
                your hands.
What would I do without the whisper of your words,
if your silken hair
were not spread out on my pillow,
if your heart did not beat upon my heart.
What would I do if my hands could not caress
your hair and your body,
if you could not hear my songs and my poems.
What would I do if my eyes could no longer
                gaze upon your image.

Arnoldo Toribio
(Paralyzed in battle with Contra forces)
Poetry Workshop of the Gaspar Garcia Laviana Rehabilitation Center

NOHEMY

Qué haría yo si me faltara
          el calor de tu boca
          tus manos.
Qué haría si tus palabras no susarraran,
si tu cabeza de cabellos lacios
no se arrecostara en mi almohada,
si tu corazón no palpitara encima del mío.
Qué haría yo si mis manos no pudieran acariciar
tus cabellos y tu cuerpo,
si mi canto y poemas no los escucharas.
Qué haría si mis ojos dejaran de contemplar tu figura.

About the Translator

Kent Johnson worked in Nicaragua in 1980 and 1983, as a teacher in the National Literacy Campaign and as an adult education instructor. He has revisited the country since then, gathering these poems and interviewing members of the Sandinista government, including Father Ernesto Cardenal, poet and Minister of Culture.

Johnson was featured in the documentary film about the Literacy Campaign, "Five Months that Changed a Nation," which was awarded a silver medal at the International Film Festival in New York in 1983. Upon his return to the United States, he received an MA degree in creative writing from the University of Wisconsin at Milwaukee in 1985. He continues to live and work in Milwaukee, where he is active in organizations for peace and freedom in Central America.